What Colour Is This?

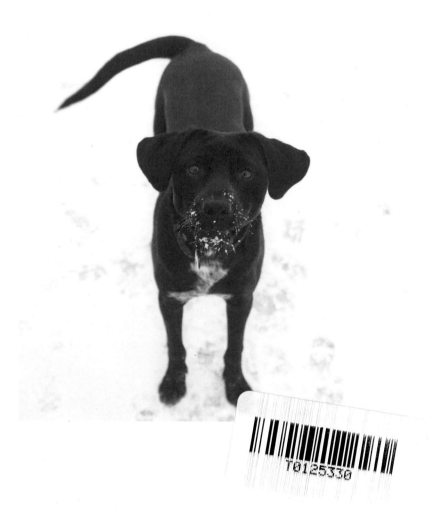

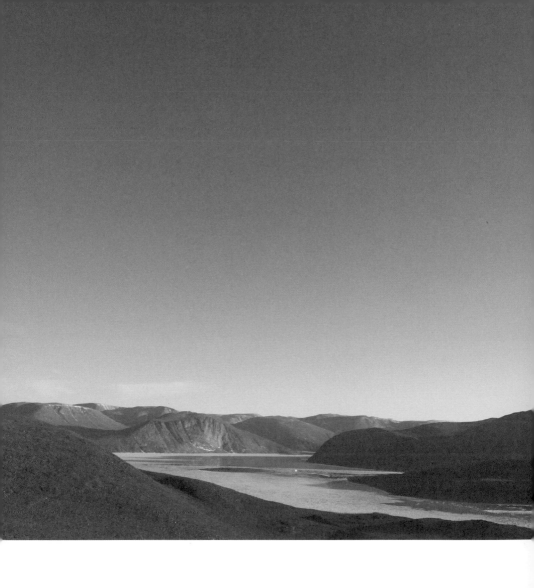

The sky is blue.

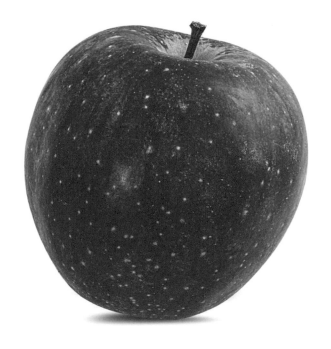

The apple is red.

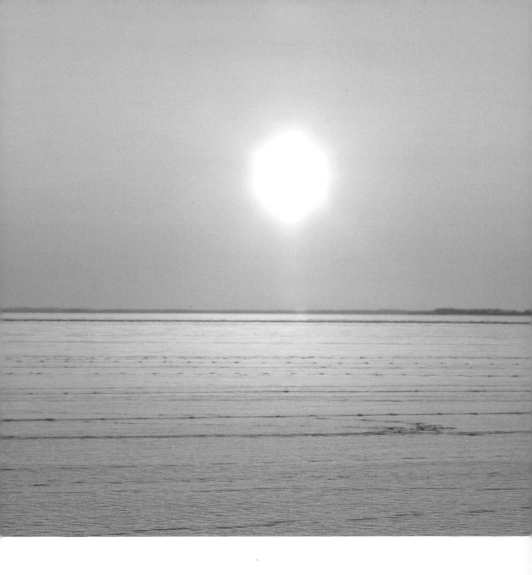

The sun is yellow.

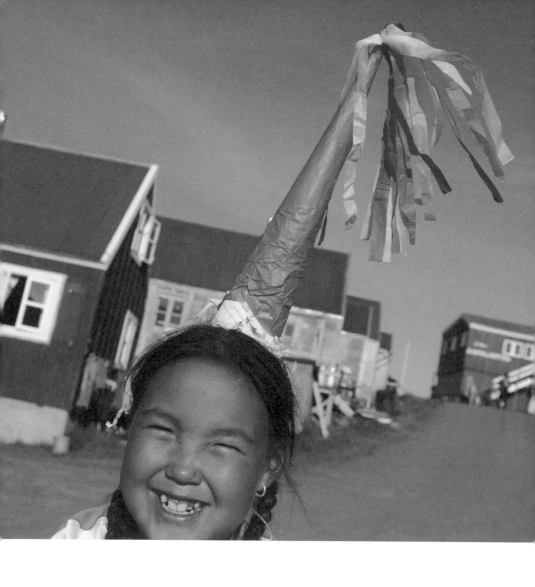

The hat is pink.

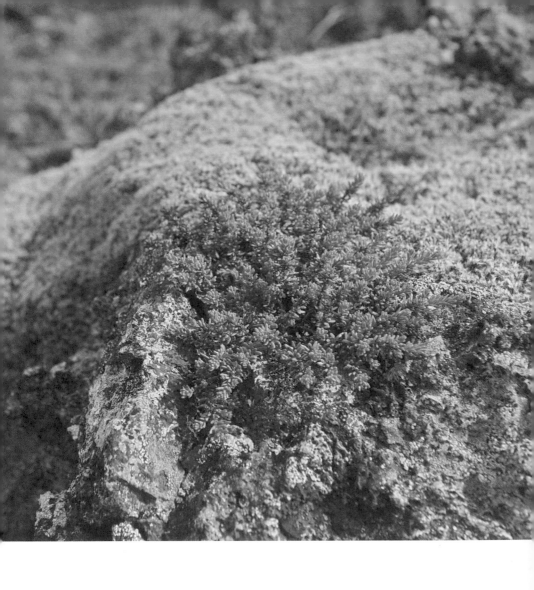

The plant is green.

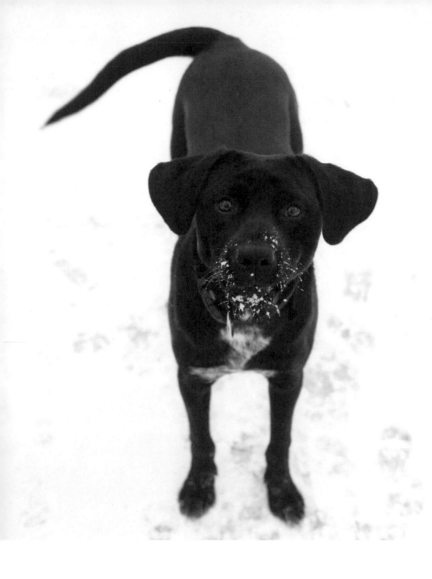

The dog is black.

The snow is white.

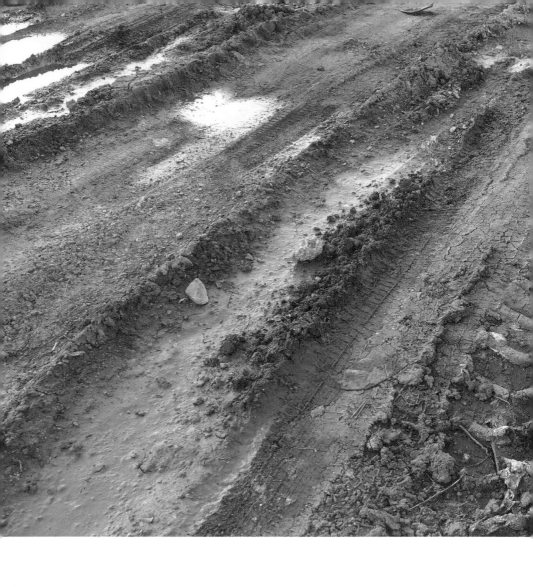

The mud is brown.

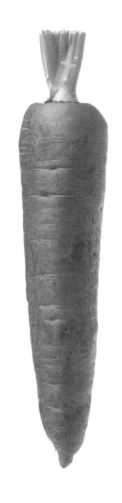

The carrot is orange.

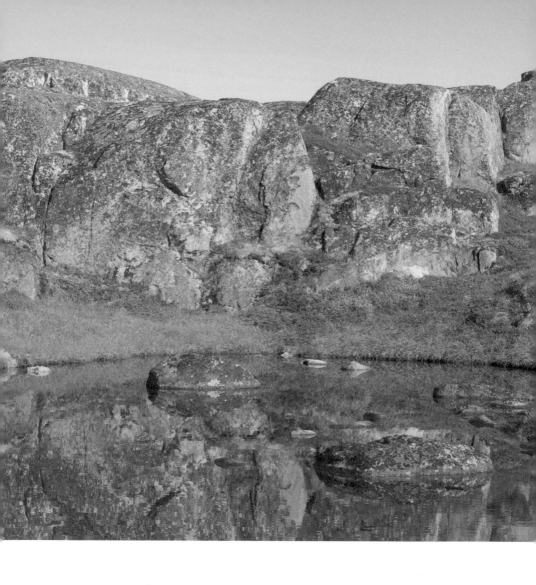

The rocks are grey.

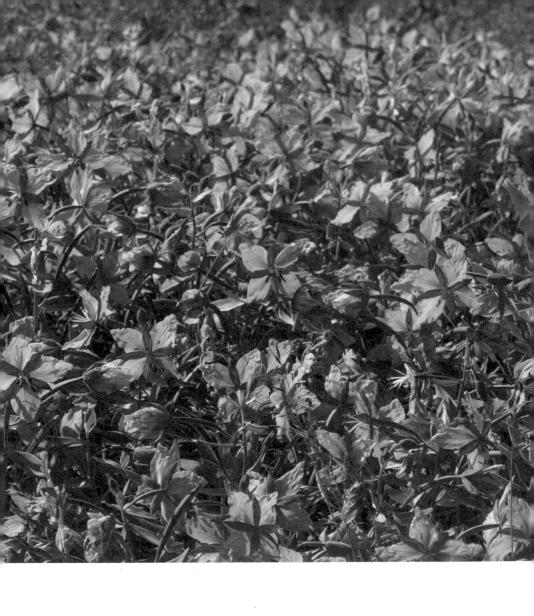

The flowers are purple